ISAVASYA ℩

Translation by Dr Latha Pillai

TURYA CHAITANYA

Isavasya Upanishad

Turya Chaitanya

(Disciple of Swami Dayananda Saraswati)

Arsha Vidya Bhushan, Kochi, Kerala, India, 682024

turyachaitanya@gmail.com

Translated by Dr Latha Pillai.

Transcribed by Ramakrishnan Karivallur

.

Dedication

I place this small commentary at the holy feet of H.H. Swami Dayananda Saraswati whose Grace has enabled me to complete this work. I personally thank Dr Latha Pillai, Ms Jennifer Catto, Sri Ramakrishnan Karivallur, Dr Mini G Pillai and Smt Ganga Ramamurthy for the successful completion of this work.

Turya Chaitanya

.

Foreword

I am very happy to recommend this book, Swami Turya Chaitanya's commentary on the Isavasya Upanishad. Here, Swamiji highlights a sweeping overview of the teachings and wisdom available to us all via the Vedas, including Vedanta and the Upanishads.

Jennifer Catto

Writer and Student of Vedanta
United states

Foreword to Malayalam edition by

Swami Dayananda saraswati

Swami Dayananda Ashram, Rishikesh

www.dayananda.org

FOREWORD

I am very happy to know that Turya Chaitanya is bringing out a book in Malayalam containing the translation and commentary on Isavasyopanisad. Being in the body of the Samhita of Sukla Yajurveda, Isavasyopanisad is a complete Vedanta Sastra. Besides unfolding the Vastu, it discusses also about Karma and Upasana, whose value for human growth has no replacement. I congratulate Turya for this service to the mumukshus and pray that the book reaches the hands of all Malayalam knowing knowledge seekers

Sd/-

SWAMI DAYANANDA SARASWATI

Preface

OM SRI GURUBHYO NAMAH

Spiritual study is the discovery of the true and the eternal in the nature of man who is a spiritual being. We are not born accidentally, and we have received this life after passing through several lives. Spiritual study will help us in this present life and also in the lives to come. Further, knowing about the Self and God realization will release us from further births. To understand about the glory of God, the study of upanishads is a must. And, as Sri Narayana Guru says, to get the divine grace of God, you have to continuously direct the mind to the feet of the Lord. A true devotee should fix the mind on the Lord, worship with steadfastness, and be endowed with supreme faith.

Devotion is of two types. One is devotion without knowledge, or Jnana, the other is devotion with knowledge of the Lord. Knowing the Lord would mean knowing the manifestations and glory of the Lord in everything we see in this universe, without and within. We come to know little bit about the Lord by intuition, and also by reading the Puranas and folklore, learning history of the various places like Ayodhya and Mathura which are directly connected to Sri Rama and Sri Krishna, and then doing meditation with or without a teacher etc. This kind of knowledge of Isvara even though it is not complete, is enough to maintain belief and worship.This is called aapata Jnanam or aapatita Jnanam meaning knowledge without much inquiry. Only when this knowledge is complete with the backing of scriptural study will we be able to submit ourselves with complete devotion. That is the bhakti of a Jnani, it is called Para bhakti. Krishna says among the four types of bhaktas, He and jnani are one and the same (Gita 7.16)

To dedicate oneself to God, the question arises, to which God should I pray? To live

7

peacefully in this world, we should fill our minds with thoughts of the Lord, do pooja, sing hymns of the Lord, and read scriptures. All this should be done regularly and with sincerity, devotion, and dedication.

Death is an inevitable part of life. There is a specific period on this earth for all of us and in this short time, what is important is how we live in this world. The choice is ours, we can lead a peaceful life radiating goodness and peace in the society, or lead a troubled, harsh life creating problems in the society. Creating problems for others will only boomerang. The condition of our mind and intellect at the time of death will invariably follow us into the next life. Our aim should be to be able to leave this world happily and peacefully. We should strive for the same with intense love and faith in God. This will influence our passage into the other worlds after death.

Thinking of death is its certainty. We have seen that our grandparents, parents and relatives and friends have passed on. We expect life to give us happiness, fulfillment and peace but it is not so. As the years go by, we realize that the prime time of life has passed, and we have not attained peace or fulfillment. Life is really a series of experiences, in the meantime we have the opportunity to gain spiritual knowledge. The more we are attached to our worldly objects, the more we feel depressed at the time of death.

Relationships are also all temporary, just a passing phase. We see parents abandoned in old age homes, temples, streets and on the roads. We get angry with others, because they do not fulfill our expectations and make us happy. They have come into this world to complete their Karma and find their own happiness, not ours, but we are trying to squeeze happiness out of them. When we live for happiness,we should not hurt the feelings of other individuals.

Vedas

We all want to live a life of joy and peace in the world. For this, devotion to God is necessary. The barrier to this is our mind which is filled with troublesome and unnecessary thoughts. These have to be replaced with godly thoughts. But how is this possible? This is possible by study of the Vedas.

The Vedas tell us about the origin of the universe, the origin of man, the philosophy of life and death, the do's and don'ts of life, and how to know the Supreme Lord. The Vedas have originated from Brahman, the absolute reality itself. The four Vedas are Rigveda, Yajurveda, Samaveda and Atharvaveda.

Each Veda has four subdivisions Samhitas, Aranyakas, Brahmanas and Upanishads. The term Veda means knowledge. They also explain about the Supreme Power and the means to attain Moksha, liberation from a life of samsara, a life of suffering.

Upanishads

There are about 1180 upanishads. Of these, the most important are the ten upanishads known as Dashopanishads. The first of these is the Isavasya Upanishad. By studying the Isavasya Upanishad we are taking a decisive step to enter the world of spirituality.

The upanishads require close study. They must be read again and again at every step of mental maturity. The words of the upanishads come from the depths of truth. Upanishads tell us about the Atman, the Self which abides in the heart of everyone. His presence should radiate through speech, mind and intellect.

The only solution to how to live life to the fullest is the study of upanishads. With true knowledge, we can overcome the shortcomings of life and raise ourselves to greater heights. A spiritual seeker who reads the upanishads will feel that he's dealing with a theme that is very close to his life and destiny, which is actually the truth of himself and the world outside. The path to overcome our deficiencies and miseries is a study of the Vedas. Upanishads are the cream of the Vedas. Isavasya upanishad, being the first among the ten major upanishads, is considered one of the oldest upanishad and very important. This is a part of Yajur Veda. Yajur Veda has two parts Krishna Yajur Veda and Shukla Yajurveda. Isa Vasya Upanishad is a part of Shukla yajurveda. It contains 18 mantras. It is also called Vajasaneya Samhita Upanishad. The first mantra starts with the word Isavasyam, hence it is called Isavasya Upanishad.

Several questions have been asked by man since time immemorial. What is the basis of the universe? What is the truth ? Where did I come from? "Where am I going? What is death? What happens after death? What is happiness? What is misery? Why do we all have to suffer? Are we born to suffer? How did the universe originate? What is the basis of the existence of the universe? What is the true meaning of "I." Man searches for answers. The

Upanishads will act as a beacon, a lighthouse for all those who step into the ocean of Life.

Santi mantra

ॐ पूर्णमदः पूर्णमिदं पूर्णात्पूर्णमुदच्यते

पूर्णस्य पूर्णमादाय पूर्णमेवावशिष्यते

ॐ शान्तिः शान्तिः शान्तिः

Om

purnamada: purnam idam

Purnat purnam udacyate

Purnasya purnam adaya

Purnam evavasisyate

Om   = Symbol of
Absolute
                                        Reality
Purnam ada: = The Brahman is
                                        complete

Purnam idam world	=This phenomenal is complete
Purnat and	= from that full complete
Purnam udachyathe world	= This complete arises
Purnasya purnam adaya jagat (world)	= remove the from the Brahman
Purnam eva avasisyathe purna	= what remains is (Brahma) alone

Brahman or Sat is perfect and complete. So all emanations from Brahman, such as the apparent phenomenal world, are also complete. Even if we cognitively remove the world from Brahman, what remains is Brahman, which is complete.

Mantra 1

ईशावास्यमिदंसर्वंयत्किंचजगत्यांजगत्।

तेन त्यक्तेन भुञ्जीथा मा गृधः कस्य

स्विद्धनम्

Isavasyamidam sarvam
Yat kinca jagathyam jagath
Tena thyakthena bhunjitha
Ma grdhah kasya swid dhanam

Yat kinch idam	= this
Sarvam	= entire

Jagatyam jagat	= world that is continuously changing, moving
Isa vasyam	= should be covered by Isvara

Tena tyaktena   = by this renunciation

Bhunjeeta: = you may enjoy

Ma grudha   = should not grab(covet)

Kasyasvid dhanam= another person's wealth

Isa means the Lord. He pervades the whole universe. One who doesn't realize this will see everything in this universe as objects of pleasure or pain. If we can perceive the universe as a manifestation of God, the view will be totally different. Live in this world and enjoy it with a spirit of devotion, also by not harming others. This is the meaning of the mantra. Tena thyaktena bhunjitha: ma grudha: kasyaswid dhanam, do not covet others wealth. Be satisfied with your possession.

Mantra 2

कुर्वन्नेवेहकर्माणिजिजीविषेच्छतंसमाः

एवं त्वयि नान्यथेतोऽस्ति न कर्म लिप्यते नरे

2

kurvanneveha Karmaṇi

jijīviṣet śataṁ samāḥ,

evaṁ tvayi nānyatheto'sti

na Karma lipyate nare

Kurvan	= performing
Karmani	= action
Eva	= alone
Iha	= during this span of life
Jijiviset satam	= desire to live one hundred
Samaa:	= years
Evam	= in this manner
Tvayi Nare	= unto you man
Asti	= there is
Na	= not
Anyadha:	= another way
Karma	= Karma
Na Lipyate	= does not bind

In this life one might desire to live for a 100 years, but only by performing actions. We can see that life on this earth has meaning and significance, by remembering constantly that God pervades the whole universe. Be fixed in this knowledge. Always be aware of our sense organs and our actions that follow desires. Creating awareness in all our actions should be our priority.

Dedicate all our actions to God. This will help us to lead a peaceful, healthy and happy life free of miseries. Sri Krishna explains to Arjuna thus-

'Lokesmin dvividha nishta

Pura prokta Mayanakha

Jnana yogena sankyanam

Karmayogena yoginam' (B.G.3.3)

There are two committed lifestyles about which I have spoken earlier. They are Jnana yoga for sankhyas (sanyasis) and Karma yoga for yogis.

It is very difficult to understand the inner meaning of this sloka. Purification of the mind is essential to grasp the higher knowledge of the Self. Our mind is a flow of thoughts gushing in, one after the other. The quality of our thoughts depends upon the nature of the mind. Even if we keep quiet outwardly, our mind is full of thoughts. Depending on our thoughts, we pursue the world outside. It might be a new spiritual sadhana, or a new business, or a new job. We might try to become rich, etc. Thus living an outwardly directed life, we fail to realize the purpose of our life. We fail to realize who we really are, and this binds us to the cycle of birth and death. This is ascertained in the next mantra.

Mantra 3

असुर्यानामतेलोकाअन्धेनतमसावृताः

तांस्ते प्रेत्याभिगच्छन्ति ये के चात्महनो जनाः

asuryā nāma te lokā:
andhena tamasā vṛtāḥ,
tāṁs te pretyābhigacchanti
ye ke cātmahano janāḥ

Asurya Nama = famous by the name

Asurya

Te = those

Lokah	= worlds
Aandhena tamasa	= by the darkness which
	has the nature of non revealing
Avratah	= covered
Tante pratya abhigachanti	= they enter into that
	after death
Ye ke cha	= all of those persons
	are
Atma hano Janah	= destroyers of self.

'ye ke cātmahano janāḥ' indicates those who are ignorant of their own essential true nature. Our true nature is not what we see in the mirror. In the Upanishads, the Rishis speak of our own true nature which is called Atma. Those who are not aware of their own true nature are called slayers of

20

the Atma. "Brahma satyam, Jagat mithya", Brahman is Atma. Atma is the conscious principle in man which illuminates all his faculties including his intellect. Atma is eternal. Atma is not born. Atma does not die. Atma is pure existence.

What is our aim in life? Why have we come to the world? We have come for a special cause. If we have come only to eat, drink, and procreate, what is the difference between man and animal? There are innumerable creatures on this earth. Their life is programmed. They cannot alter their life pattern. They are content with their lives, as they do not have ambitions. But what about us? Man has wisdom and insight. He can deliberate on his thoughts and make intelligent decisions. He can reflect on his own existence and the existence of everyone. He can wonder about the Atman or consciousness. Those who do not do so are called "ye ke cātmahano janāḥ"

Life lived without being conscious of our divine nature is trivial. It is a life of darkness and sorrow, of ignorance. It is otherwise called spiritual blindness. Let us not be like this. Understanding our inner reality should be our goal. We have to master our inner lives, train ourselves to live a life of self-mastery. That is religion. Disciplining the mind and intellect would lead to strengthening of the psychological and intellectual abilities.

Citing an example, the Kumbhamela is a major pilgrimage festival in Hinduism. The festival is marked by a ritual dip in the Ganga or Narmada river. It is attended by saints, monks, sadhus, ascetics and pilgrims from all walks of life. The Mela draws tens of millions of pilgrims and many others like merchants and various service people. In spite of all this, if any person has an unpleasant experience, all sanyasis are blamed. If one politician is caught for bribery, the whole political party is blamed. So people have the tendency to exaggerate the problems of others and create confusion. Blaming others for our faults is a hobby for many. We believe that we have no faults. To clean the mind of such confusions purification of mind is necessary."Chittashudhi".

This is possible by close study of Upanishads and realizing the Atman. Karma Yoga and Upasana purifies the mind, and the purified mind can gain knowledge of Self through Jnana yoga.

Mantra 4.

अनेजदेकंमनसोजवीयोनैनद्देवाआप्नुवन्पूर्वमर्षत्

तद्धावतोऽन्यानत्येति तिष्ठ—तस्मिन्नपो

मातरिश्वा दधाति 4

anejad ekaṁ manaso javīyo

nainad devā āpnuvan pūrvamarṣat,

tad dhāvato'nyān=atyeti tiṣṭhat

tasminn apo mātariśvā dadhāti

Anejad	=fixed
Ekam	= one
Manasah	= than the mind
Javeeya	= swifter
Enat	= this Supreme Lord
Deva:	= Devas
Na	= not

Apnuvan	= gained, approached
Purvam	= earlier
Arsat	= moving quickly
Tat	= he
Dhavato	= those who are running
Anyan	= others
Atyeti	= surpasses
Tisthat	= remaining in one place
Tasmin	= in that
Matarisva	= Prana, Vayu
Apo adhati	= separates Karma

The Self is motionless, and yet it is also said here to be swifter than the mind. The Devas [sense organs] cannot overtake the Self. It supports the activity of all beings. Ejath - motionless. Ekam - one. Manaso javeeyo - faster than the mind. Poorvam arshath - going in front. The Atma is faster than the mind and goes in front. Atma, Brahman, Isvara are all one and the same. Even the Devas cannot realize the Atman. The Devas means that which are self illumined, effulgent. The five sense organs of

24

perception are the capacity to hear, touch, see, taste and smell. Through these we perceive the entire world. In Hindu scriptures the Devas control the functioning of the Universe and are called the presiding deities. Our sense organs are illuminated by the Devas. So the sense organs are also called Devas. The Sun is called 'vishvasya chakshu'. The Sun is the presiding deity of the eyes. The eyes are able to see because of the blessings of the Sun. So also the other sense organs. The fields of experience are hearing, touch, sight,taste and smell. The sense organs along with physical instruments were used to study the mysteries of the universe. There is a limit to what can be seen directly, and we have to use our inference to know about other galaxies. Our mind can reach anywhere according to our imagination. Whatever or which place we think, Atma is very much there even before the thought of that place or object arises. Figuratively, Atma reaches there earlier. For our eyes to see, there should be someone giving the power to sense organs to see. Our mind goes after objects of desire. This is possible because of the Atma. But Atma doesn't go after the object. That is the difference.

The Atma is considered as the true reality or Sat. The Atma resides in the heart of all living beings as Sri Krishna told Arjuna in the Bhagavad Gita. 'Hrudheshe rjuna thishtati, ' Isvara resides in the heart or mind of everyone. That's why the Atma is called 'AntarAtma'. The Atma is a silent spectator observing the mind. He is called 'anejat' the one who does not move, because there is no one else like him. He is the illuminator of the Devas. He is faster than all and yet does not move. Our mind goes after Wealth, Job, luxuries etc,, anything which gives us pleasure. When these are given priority in our thoughts, Atma illuminates these thoughts and they carry forward. But Atma doesn't change thoughts. Atma is just an onlooker and it is seated as the inner soul. The Atma illuminates the finite experiences. The Atman, or self, is changeless and eternal. The tricks of the mind are its own creation (Atma is beyond transaction, these are Maya's creation). The Self (Atma) is something other than the mind. Self gives awareness to the mind.

We are immersed in different types of Karma daily, Karmas are done with the help of the karmendriyas. The air we breathe regulates the energy needed for Karma, that's Prana. The Karmas are illuminated by the Jivatma but not involved in them, good or bad.

Mantra 5

तदेजतितन्नैजतितद्दूरेतद्वन्तिके

तदन्तरस्य सर्वस्य तद् सर्वस्यास्य बाह्यतः 5

Tad ejati tan naijati
tad dūre tadvantike
tad antarasya sarvasya
tad u sarvasyāsya bāhyataḥ

Tad	= that (Atma)
Ejati	= moves
Tad na ejati	= that does not move

Tad dure	= that is far away
Tad antike	= that is near
Tad Antah	= that is within
Asya	= of this
Sarvasya	= of all
Bahyato	= external to
Tad sarvasya	= of all

"This Atma moves and does not move. It is far away but also very near. It is within everything and yet it is outside of everything."

Atman or Brahman is the reality called Sat which has come to manifest itself within the body. Brahman is the ultimate reality. This Brahman moves but does not move. This idea cannot be understood very easily. If we can understand, our life would become complete. Death would be fearless. We will then be able to understand death. Our mind would be at peace always, unaffected whatever be the circumstances (Na ejaty).

We can run with our body, but our thoughts can be still. We can keep our body still, but our thoughts are running around haphazardly. Thousands of thoughts rise in our mind daily. These thoughts drain our energy and we feel tired. But it is not so in one who has realized the truth. He may be very busy but his mind is calm and he is at peace. He has understood that the Jivatma has come from the ParamAtma and will eventually go back to him. The origin and termination of the universe is from the same ParamAtma.

'Tad antarasya sarvasya' Inside, outside, near, far, he is present – Paramatma. He is the source of all energy. The one, all pervading. He is inside and outside of all beings. This statement can confuse us. If we discard the name and form of all beings what remains is only the 'Truth'. Upanishad tries to reveal this ultimate Truth which we have to grasp by studying in depth.

In the first mantra we saw about the all pervading nature of Atman and about leading a pure meditative life with detachment. In the second mantra we learn about doing our Karma with a sense of offering to Isvara. Only this will deliver us from misery.

"Tad ejathi tad na ejathy" It is moving and also still. "tad dure tad antike" It is far but also near. This is a bit difficult to comprehend. How can our mind grasp the meaning of these two mantras? It is easier to know about God with form and name like Sri Rama, Sri Krishna, and Siva and other Devas. Being near and far at the same time is confusing.

The third mantra says it is inside of all beings and outside at the same time. How is it possible? It is possible because of Maya. Maya is something that appears to exist but does not exist. If we can realize this, our life will become meaningful, otherwise we are called Atmahanta, destroyers of Self

What is Atma? Who is Atmahanta? Atma is not the one that comes to frighten us in the disguise of a ghost or the one for whom 'Bali' (a particular Karma performed to please departed souls or ancestors) is done. Here Atma is the Self or

Consciousness, which resides in the core of the heart. The answer to the question of Who I am? Is it the Atma we know? what is Atma but we have not realized or recognized it. We are not leading our lives in that knowledge. In the Purusha suktam, it says "atya tishtat dashangulam". Paramatma is depicted as enveloping the entire universe and transcending it by ten fingers length i.e, in all ten directions. This cannot be seen with our eyes. This fact has to be analyzed and understood by our intellect as it is not comprehended by our sense organs.

The five sense organs of perception are ears to hear,skin to touch, eyes to see, tongue to taste, and nose to smell. With these sense organs, we perceive the entire world, yet we cannot understand the limitless conscious existence that is Brahman so we think that this is different from the 'I' and we feel that we can't reach there. But the truth is, we are That. This understanding cannot be achieved by simply listening to talks without dwelling on what they say. Understanding can be achieved by study of the suktas (mantras, hymns) from a teacher (Guru) as in the days of the Rishis.

This has been explicitly referred to by Sri Narayana Guru in Sivasathakom – 4th sloka

"Sanakasananda Sanatkumar mumbam

Munijanamodupadeshamothi munnam

Kanivodu thekku mukham thirinju kallal,

Tharayilirunnu murthy kathukolka"

Sanaka etc were Munis who were given this knowledge by Lord Dakshinamoorthy. Muni is the sage who is in deep contemplation. He is the one who has understood the nature of the silence that lies beyond all words. Sri Dakshinamoorthy is an incarnation of Bhagavan Shiva. The knowledge of the Rishis is passed down to the students. This can be studied only from this lineage.

Sri Narayana Guru in his Chit jada chinthanam, in the fifth sloka, says

"Akhilarkum athingane thanne matam

Sukha sadhyam ithennu shukadikalum

Pakarunu paramparayay palatum

Bhagavanude Mayayaho valute."

This sloka stresses the importance of learning from the lineage of gurus.

To realize this knowledge, one must approach a Guru and listen to him. Listening would mean learning with attention. Understand that everything we come into this world is Maya. The world itself is the effect of Maya. We must be able to differentiate between Maya and the Truth. This is called sruti Jnanam, because it is learnt by listening.

For any knowledge to be gained there are several means.

1.direct perception, pratyaksham =with our all sense organs

2.inference, anumanam. eg. Smoke indicates fire.

3.Word, shabdam = scriptures, reading and listening.

When we learn from our gurus, the most important is sraddha [acceptance of scripture as valid means of knowledge.] We must study very carefully and with full concentration and commitment, like walking on a knife's edge [Kshurasya dhara]. Our vision should be directed inward –[Jnana chakshus] –eye of insight or third eye.

The flute is just a bamboo with holes. One who has learned to play can produce enchanting tunes like Sri Krishna. Attaining knowledge of the Self from Gurus by listening and contemplation is called Jnana sadhana and devotion [Bakthi] goes along with it. We can approach our Lord with love and bhakthi. As Sri Narayana guru said in his 'Chit jada chinthanam'. In the 9th sloka guru says:

"Puthumamkani poothamrithe gulame
Madhuve madhurakaniye rasa me
Vidhi Madhavaradi thiranjidumen
Pathiye padapankajame gatiye"

Our love and devotion to God should be pure and sweet like a Ripe Mango, Jaggery (a type of unrefined sugar) and Honey. Submit everything to

34

the feet of the Lord. Do all your responsibilities as worship of the Lord and consider the result as a gift from Isvara. This attitude will clean our intellect and mind. It is extremely difficult to calm the mind. Our mind is a continuous flow of thoughts. Our response to the external world depends on the nature and quality of our thoughts. One moment we are happy and the next moment we are sad. This can be compared to a boat without a rudder in the sea which moves up and down according to the direction of the wind and waves. If we want to improve the quality of our thoughts it has to be applied to the higher knowledge by reading, listening to talks, contemplation etc. We can replace our thoughts with mantras, Japa, bhajans, etc. Think deeply into the meaning of the mantras. Understand that the Supreme power will give us strength. We all have a notion [sankalpa] that there is a beautiful world out there called heavens devoid of misery. These sankalpas, imaginations are formed in our mind. When we look into the origin of the sankalpas we realize that it is the capacity of our mind to imagine the way we want it. Mind resides in me only. And I am Consciousness. So whatever we see in this world, or imagine, is in Consciousness only. Even the heavens are in me. Hence is the meaning of the sloka " tat doore, tad antike". However far our mind goes, that is also in Consciousness. "Tad antarasya sarvasya " It is inside all. To say that the whole world is in my Consciousness is very difficult to comprehend.

Spiritual practice of contemplation is not holding one's breath or prana. It is not imagining a bright light inside me. Or controlling the mind. Physically; yoga, pranayama, japa are all beneficial for our body-mind complex but only spiritual study along with Karma yoga and devotion leads to true understanding of our own nature, and to liberation.

There are three states- waking, dreaming and sleeping. The range of human experience is wide and varied. The physical world is experienced by the five sense organs. In the waking state, the entire personality is awake and functioning and experiences the world. In the dream state, the mind creates and sustains the dream world. In the deep sleep state, we do not know anything and give up identification with the body. How can the experiences in the waking state be lost in the dream state and yet also be real? Also, the experiences in the dream state are lost when awakened. In the deep sleep state there is absence of any experience. What is not lost in all three states is the Atman. This is the basis of Upanishads.

Bhakti helps in cleaning our intellect and mind. This will help to reduce the thoughts and sharpen the mind. To lead a peaceful life good sankalpas (thoughts) are needed. It is easy to believe in Supreme power with a form like Devis and Devas to begin with, as suggested by the puranas (a group of texts like Srimad Bhagavatam,shiva purana etc). A cruel person or a criminal can also present himself or herself as a spiritual person to the society by wearing religious symbols. That person is a real enemy of spirituality and association with that type of person should be avoided. Even the demon king Ravana was presented as a devotee of Shiva and as one who is an expert in Sama Veda. It is not that all bhaktas are good. In the end Ravana was killed by Sri Rama.

In Sivamanasa Pooja, Adi Sankaracharya illustrates this:

ātmā tvaṃ girijā matiḥ sahacharāḥ prāṇāḥ śarīraṃ gṛhaṃ

pūjā te viśhayopabhoga=rachanā nidrā samādhisthitiḥ

sañchāraḥ padayoḥ pradakśhiṇavidhiḥ stotrāṇi sarvā giro

yadyatKarma karomi tattadakhilaṃ śambho tavārādhanam

" Oh Parameswara! You are the Atma and Girija (Parvaty) is the buddhi, intelligence. The vital energies [Prana] are your companions. This body (shareeram) is your house. Worship of you is enjoyment of vishayas (objects of enjoyment). Sleep is the state of Samadhi. Wandering is the ceremony of circumambulation. All my words [girah] are hymns of praise. Whatever action I do is your adoration Oh! Samboh [Siva]."

Saguna upasana (Aradhana) is virtuous but our Rishis stress on learning the truth of Isvara from a guru. This would require close proximity to a guru along with mantra deeksha or initiation into the study. Mantra deeksha is the traditional way of accepting a student by a teacher and making an individual to be qualified for the pursuit of Vedic knowledge by which the ultimate goal of life can be achieved. This is to be followed by close practice and contemplation. Only continuous study, contemplation and devotion can help to reach the goal.

Bhagavad Gita 4th ca. 34th sloka says,

tad viddhi praṇipātena pariprashnena sevayā

upadekṣhyanti te Jnanaṁ jñāninas tattvadarshinaḥ

Learn the truth by approaching a spiritual master. Inquire with reverence and render service unto him. Such an enlightened saint can impart knowledge unto you because he has seen the truth.

How can we attain spiritual knowledge? Bhagavan Sri Krishna gives the answer in this verse. The absolute truth cannot be understood by our own contemplation.

One who has no inclination to acquire this knowledge goes after objects of desire and falls into the pit of misery. They lose their 'sat' (truth) svarupa knowledge about themselves and are called Atma hanta. They reach dark worlds where there is no Sun. By Sun it is meant the knowledge of Atman. One without Atmajnanam goes after worldly desires. When he gets one desire fullfilled the next one will pop up. He rushes to acquire that. He is also afraid to lose what he has got. Such a person without the knowledge of Atman is said to live in a dark world without peace. He is always restless and never satisfied.

What do we have to lose in this world? People come and go. Similarly, objects are acquired and lost. It's a cycle of birth and death. What do we have to lose when we all become old? Children have to be taught Sanskrit slokas, bhajans, spiritual stories, etc. Vedanta should be taught to older mature children, if they show interest. Do not force it on them. And one can start learning the moment one is interested, irrespective of their age.

How do we know that we have realized the Atman? During meditation, there may be a feeling of tightening body parts, or electric shock-like sensations, or numbness, or lack of breath. None of these are signs of realization; it is simply our body permeated by the pranas. When we know the all-pervading, inside and outside, moving and not moving Truth(ParamAtma,) we truly understand the Lord. This is Atman. This is the message of all Upanishads. We may have understood it but to bring it into our life is very difficult.

Attaining spiritual knowledge doesn't mean getting good experiences. The experiences are dependent on the sense organ. These cannot be changed. E.g. Fire is hot. Salt is salty. Do not expect that fire does not burn the finger of a Jnani. Yet he who knows the Brahman which words cannot express, mind cannot reach, he is free from fear.

Mantra 6

यस्तुसर्वाणिभूतानिआत्मन्येवानुपश्यति

सर्वभूतेषु चात्मानं ततो न विजुगुप्सते 6

Yastu sarvani bhutani

Atmany evanupasyathy

Sarva bhutheshu chatmanam

Tato na vijugupsate

Ya: tu	= he who
Anupasyati	= sees, knows, observes
Sarvani bhutani	= all living entities
Atmani	= in Atma
Eva	= only
Atmanam cha	= and one self
Sarvabhuteshu	= in every living being
Tata:	= thereafter
Na	= not

42

Vijugupsate   = hates anyone

"He who sees everything in ParamAtma and ParamAtma in everything, never hates any being thereafter."

The quality of a person's knowledge of the truth of himself can be judged by his behaviour with others. If we see others as enemies it would mean that we do not see the Atman in them. Lord Sri Krishna could play the flute sweetly for the Gopikas but at the same time he was harsh with Jarasanda and Narakasura. Both times he was at peace within. A man of realization does not get frustrated at any commissions or omissions in life. The Atma is all pervading and unbounded.

The Atma or Brahman pervades all living beings in the universe. The universe is seen by all in the waking state. In the dream state we see another world. Where does all this disappear in the deep sleep state? Who is present in all three states? That is the Supreme Consciousness in all living beings.

Atma is explained as available in the heart. That means I am aware of my heart, I am aware of my body. I am aware of my surroundings. I am aware of my mind. Every living and nonliving being comes under my awareness. Whatever there is in the whole universe comes under my consciousness. That consciousness is Atma. This is the meaning of Sarva bhuteshu chatmanam.

Hence the 'I', the Supreme consciousness, in all beings in the universe is the same. There is nothing to separate Paramatma. Being the Paramatma, nothing separates me from anything. There is nothing like giving and taking when all have the same consciousness. This is the most important part of spiritual knowledge. It cannot be understood at the level of the mind.

All beings are pervaded by the Atma or consciousness. The different beings are the different names and forms taken by the consciousness. This Advaita philosophy is called Vedanta. Advaita means non dichotomous, non dual. This is not an ordinary thing to understand. Only repeated listening, learning and contemplation of the Upanishads in the presence of a Guru will help. Seeing the oneness in all living and nonliving things, will help release us from all the miseries of life.

In Bhagavad Gita it is said, do not lament over those who are dead. Sri Krishna told Arjuna, in this world there are only two groups of people. One in whom all are dead. And the other group in which all are destined to die. One who is alive is in turn waiting for his card, and he is only a sakshi (witness) to those who are dying.

Love and devotion are all values. These values cannot be sidelined or neglected. With the help of these values one can study scriptures and think of ParamAtma. The study elevates us to a higher level. Both Sri Krishna and Sri Rama in their lives have been shown to uplift human values. One who is attached to worldly affairs, like family, etc. may go weak and sad in times of despair. This is seen in all Puranas as it illustrates the life stories of bhaktas. Whereas when one doesn't feel sad or attached to one's family, he may choose to seek spiritual knowledge, leaving home in search of a Guru and a life of seclusion. This is also illustrated in puranas. Those who are purified by Brahma Jnanam are called jnanis or munis. These munis are worthy of respect in every society.

mantra 7

यस्मिन्सर्वाणिभूतानिआत्मैवाभूद्विजानतः

तत्र को मोहः कः शोक एकत्वमनुपश्यतः 7

Yasmin sarvani bhutani

Atmaivabhut vijanatah

Tatra ko moha:ka:shoka:

Ekatvamanupasyata:

Yasmin (kale)	= when
Sarvani Bhuthani	= all living entities
atmaivabhut	= exist as Atma
Tatra (tasmin kale)	= at that time

ekatvam anupashyata = the one who understands

oneness

Ko moha: =what (or where) is delusion

Ka: shoka: = what (or where) is sorrow

"This mantra conveys the same meaning as the previous mantra. When one sees all living beings as Paramatma then where is moha (delusion)and shoka(sorrow). How can he have anxiety or depression? All beings are pervaded by the Atma or consciousness. The different beings are the different names and forms taken by the consciousness. This

Advaita philosophy is called Vedanta. Advaita means non dichotomous, non dual. This is tough to understand. Only repeated listening, learning and contemplation of the Upanishads in the presence of a Guru will help. Seeing the oneness in all living and nonliving things, will help release us from all the miseries of life.

In Bhagavad Gita it is said do not lament over those who are dead. Sri Krishna told

47

Arjuna , in this world there are only two groups of people. One in whom all are dead. And the other group in which all are waiting to die. One who is alive is in turn waiting for his card and he is only a Sakshi(witness) to those who are dying.

Love and devotion are all values. These values cannot be sidelined or neglected.With the help of these values one can study scriptures and think of Paramatma. The study elevates us to a higher level. Both Sri Krishna and Sri Rama in their lives have been shown to uplift human values. When one is attached to worldly affairs like family etc may go weak and sad in times of despair. This is seen in all Puranas as it illustrates life stories of bhaktas. Whereas when one doesn't feel sad or attached to one's family, and seeking spiritual knowledge leaves home in search of a Guru and lives a life of seclusion, this also illustrated in puranas. Those who are purified themselves with Brahmajnanam is called a jnani or muni in olden days. These Munis are worthy of respect in every society.

Mantra 8

सपर्यगाच्छुक्रमकायमव्रण—

मस्नाविरंशुद्धमपापविद्धम्

कविर्मनीषी परिभूः स्वयम्भूर्याथातथ्यतो   —

ऽर्थान्व्यदधाच्छाश्वतीभ्यः समाभ्यः 8

sa paryagāt shukram, akāyam, avraṇam,

asnāviram, śuddham, apāpaviddham,

kavir maṇīṣī, paribhūḥ, svayambhūḥ,

yāthātathyato'rthān vyadadhāt

shāśvatībhyas samābhyaḥ

Sah	= that Atma
Paryagat	= all pervading
Shukram	= one who shines and pure
Akayam	=unembodied
Avranam	= without bruise
Asnaviram	= without nerves.
Suddham	= uncontaminated
APapavidham	= without sins

Kavir	= visionary(poet)
Maneeshi	= Supreme Lord, witness of mind
Paribhu:	= above all
Svayambhu:	= who exists by himself without a cause
Yathathatyatah	= as it is seen
Arthan	= the responsibilities (of managing the world)
Vyadhadat	= awarded
Sasvatibhyah	= to the everlasting
Samabhyah	= prajapatis

This mantra tells us about Brahman. He who is omnipresent and is self luminous. The one who is without a causal body and is free from a physical body and its parts. The one without any physical injury and the one who is not afflicted by results of bad Karma. The one who is pure and visionary, lord of the mind, He is above everything. He being the causeless cause of everything, but not an effect of anything, being Isvara, he differentiated Karma to

Prajapatis (one group of Devas, from whom all living beings came) such as Samvatsara etc.

Word by word meaning of this mantra tells us all about Brahman. 'Sa' means He, the Lord – Supreme Power. 'Paryagat' - pervading the whole universe. 'Sukram' - the one who is effulgent. 'Akayam' – one without a subtle body [absence of sookshma sareeram], he is devoid of a form. 'Avranam' - one without any injuries. 'Asnaviram' - one without nerves. It implies that he has no gross body or sthoola sareeram. 'Apapavidham' - sinless. 'Suddham' - pure and innocent. Doesn't have a causal body. 'Kavi' - one who is a visionary, a poet. 'Manishi' - witness of mind. 'Paribhu' - beyond all. 'Swayambhu' - originated by itself, not from anything. 'Yaadhaatathyatah' means the way it is to be, in real terms. Shaswateebhya samabhya: (dadati) – He alone allotted the Karma to the various everlasting Prajapatis (their respective functions are for the continuity of the world).

Prajapatis are creators of living beings and they are the rulers too. The term refers to a different group of Devas who are even fathers of Devas, like Indra etc. They are responsible for the creation. They all have a period/time [kalam] in this universe. This is divided into seconds, minutes, hours, weeks, months, and years. Anything that is created here has a future, present and a past. All these creations are possible only if there is time.

See "Time" as a concept. Time does not have a past, present or future. It is one alone. About the creator, humans came from Manu Prajapati, reptiles from another and so on. Prajapati or creator means different principles. The Supreme Lord is the cause for all creators. He is called Isvara (and ultimately) Paramatma.

'Eet' means to rule. Isvara is the one who rules the world that includes Prajapatis too. The Supreme Lord or Isvara is the One pure truth. Independent, He pervades the whole universe. Sukra means pure, and effulgent. When we say Isvara and I, there are two entities. 'The universe' and 'I', also two entities. The five elements of the universe are space, air, fire, water and earth. When we say two entities, it would mean many, like one Isvara and many Jivas counted as two or one world and many Jivas as two. The universe is made up of objects which are nothing but names and forms. When we analyse them, we realize that all are made of five elements. This knowledge helps us realize that we are one with the Supreme power. We must have a definite and a doubtless confirmation of the plurality and a firm assertion of the non-dual Brahman. The philosophy of non-dualism insists on One reality, one without a second alone is the most rational and correct.

Upanishads have an exhaustive range of literature relating to the Paramatma and Jivatma. If we think we know everything, then our spiritual study will stop. It is always better to keep searching for the Truth. Some say we have to experience the Lord. Isvara cannot be experienced with our sense organs. We must be able to see the Lord in all beings on the earth.

The three bodies are: gross Body, subtle Body and causal Body. Presently when we think of the mind, we think of the gross body. So we will start with the analysis of the gross body. Gross body gives us an identity. Each of us have different identities. Gross Body is made up of the five elements. Space, Air, Fire, Water and Earth. All of us perceive the body with the sense organs. At death, the body disintegrates into the five elements. Pervading the gross body is the subtle body. Subtle body cannot be perceived by the sense organs. When it leaves the gross body, we say that the person is dead. The causal body is the subtlest of the three and pervades the other two. It is of the nature of ignorance called Avidya. It has no size or shape. Ignorance can be destroyed only by knowledge. So ignorance is not eternal. The Self, being beyond birth and death, is eternal. I must understand myself as different from all the 3 bodies, i.e. gross, subtle and causal bodies.

On the path of study the first step is collecting information. We can teach our children also. Learn the slokas (stanza) of Gita word by word with meaning. Initially it may be difficult to study in depth. After the initial study try to analyse. Think diligently using our intelligence and try logical reasoning. Try to learn from the light of our experiences and bring an order to our studies. If the aspirants study systematically, with intelligence, they can become experts in the subject. They will have good understanding and analytical capability. They will be a storehouse of information and will be able to instruct others. Study of Vedanta can be a challenge even for the wise person. Sometimes a word's direct meaning is discarded (jahat lakshana, jahat means give up). Some words may have to be added to get the correct meaning [ajahat lakshana, ajahat means not giving up]. Some of the words used in Vedanta, we may understand only after a long period of time. Similarly, the nature of Brahman, Atma etc. while trying to understand we need Isvara's blessings and for that one can visit temples and pray to the ishta devata, pray to remove sins etc. But we should not deviate from the path of knowledge. This is attainable only by studying the scriptures in depth. Ritualistic part of the religion needs several participants and may not satisfy the present generation. What we say here is individualistic and an organised group gathering is not needed and not desirable.

In this mantra, the Paramatma is referred as Kavi and Maneeshi. Kavi means a poet, the whole universe is an art work of the Lord and he is the one who visualised this world, that's why he is called Kavi. Maneeshi is a witness. The Self is the same 'life principle' in all living beings. He is the eternal knower and witness in all beings.

Just as Vishnu's abode is Vaikuntam, others have their own too. Brahmaji's Brahmalokam, Mahadeva's Kailasom, Devas' Devalokam etc. The abode of Paramatma is everywhere. Paramatma resides everywhere in the universe. We see

Paramatma with a name and form every time we see anything. We know and see the universe through the sense organs and the rest is our beliefs. We have to understand the reality in the world of plurality with our mind and intellect. We have to accept that there is a first cause which made this world. But the ultimate cause has no other cause. So it is called 'Swayambhu' or self- sprung.

The Supreme Lord allotted the duties to the Devas. At the same time he resides in the heart of all living beings as the witness. He is always independent and is the light in all beings. Much of what has been said is difficult to comprehend. This difficulty is the first step to prove that we have started to reach Him. Next two mantras will tell us about the nature of Upasana and the courses of actions to be taken.

Mantra 9

अन्धंतमःप्रविशन्तियेअविद्यामुपासते

ततो भूय इव ते तमो य उ विद्यायां रताः 9

andhaṁ tamaḥ praviśanti

ye(a)vidyām upasate

tato bhūya iva te tamo

ya u vidyāyāṁ ratāḥ

Andam	= blind
Tama	= darkness
pravishanthi	= enter
Ye	= who
U	= verily
Upasate	= follow
Avidyam	= Avidya
Ya u Vidyayam rata:	= those who engaged in
	Vidya
Pravishanti	= enter
Tatobhuya iva te tama:	= in deep darkness,

in a more pathetic situation (world)

58

" They who worship Avidya (Karma) fall into darkness and they who worship Vidya (upasana) fall into even greater darkness."

Mantra 10

अन्यदेवाहुर्विद्यययाअन्यदाहुरविद्यया

इति शुश्रुम धीराणां ये नस्तद्विचचक्षिरे 10

anyad evāhur Vidyayā

anyad āhur Avidyayā

iti śuśruma dhīrāṇām

ye nas tad vicacakṣire

Eva	= definitely
Ahu	= They say
Vidyaya	= by Vidya
Anyad (phalam)	= different (Result)
Avidyaya	= by Avidya
Anyad	= different result
Iti	= thus
Sushruma	= we have heard
Dhiiranam	= who
Na:	= to us

Tat   = that

Vichachakshire   = explained.

Result of Avidya and the result of Vidya are different. Thus we have heard from the wise who explained that to us.

In both the mantras the Rishis explain about Vidya and Avidya and the result of following either of the paths.

Rishi says those who are following Avidya fall into darkness which blinds us, and those who are following Upasana path fall into the abyss of darkness. We are bound to perform many Karma in daily life. We visit temples daily, do japa and pooja, cater to our family members, and do housechores, cleaning, go to office etc. We believe this will bring blessings from God. Which is Vidya and which is Avidya among these?

What is Vidya? It is described as Upasana here. This meaning is applicable here only. What is not Vidya is Avidya. Karma sastra is called Avidya and Upasana sastra is called Vidya in this mantra, elsewhere meaning will be different. Our whole life is spent in doing two types of Karma, either good or bad. These will lead to good impressions or bad impressions. The agnihotri Karma or Yajnas [pancha maha yanjas] can give good impressions. These are called Avidya here. The success of any yagna being done depends on several external factors like materials, manpower, etc. Eg. If a Yajna needs wood, and wood which was used has a hollow with a snake inside, this snake would be killed by the fire of the Yajna. This would bring a devastating effect on the Yajna. A Yajna cannot be done single-handedly. To do Karma in the worldly life he should be married. If one leads a different life against the social norms he should leave the society. In our culture society demands families to follow the mores and norms. But now it is not so. Families are broken down. This destroys our culture. Our Vedas give emphasis on husband-wife relationship. Our Upanishads demand that the husbands give out the best treatment for their wives. This is the pillar of society. They should respect each other. All this has gone down the drains. Our children are not taught anything like this.

In manu smriti it is said (9 – 101)

Anyonyasya avyabhicharo Bhavet aamaranantika:

Esha Dharmassamasena Jneya ssthrepumsayo para:

This shloka explains the husband - wife relationship. The whole life should be dedicated to each other and another person should not enter their family life. There was nothing like divorce in those days. It was not needed also. Manu says both are responsible for harmony in the family.

Similarly in Santhi Parvam 144th chapter, Ezhuthachan explains about family relationships. A family with morals will have a happy atmosphere. The head of the house teaches good Karma to all family members.

"Avalillaykilo meda polum kadanu nishchayam ……"

Of the four Purusharthas, goals of mankind, it is said that for Dharma, Artha, Kama, the wife should be present. For Moksha, the wife need not be present. A man should consider his wife as his biggest wealth. Even if he is bereft of wealth, he has to take care of her well being. In his helplessness, his wife alone will be there to help. She won't abandon him. Mahabharata repeatedly emphasizes on the importance of wife. But it is not so nowadays. Because women are ill-treated in several homes, they even need protection from their own husbands. Men should see wives as the anchor of support when they are beaten by hardships of life.

For a man there is no relative greater than his wife, not even mother or father. He has to take care of her. To attain Purushartha, she has to support and be with him. But if the behavior of the wife is intolerable, always unpleasant, not attending to his needs, finding fault, criticizing his family, what is to be done? He should then leave the family and go to the forests. It is said so in the Mahabharata. It is not ideal to go for another marriage because he failed to make his wife happy. If he does not go to the forest, his house will become one. In short, an understanding, good wife is needed to build a good family.

Karma done by householders is called Avidya (Karma). If such Karma deviates from Dharma, the result can be disastrous. If the result is positive, the family can enjoy life till the merit is over. Then again, they have to toil for living a happy life. This will not give long lasting happiness. So it is said in the sloka that Avidya leads to darkness.

The next line is for Vidya. "Andham tama: pravishanty"" ya Vidyayam rata:. Those who follow Vidya go into greater darkness. Upasana[meditation], Hymns, Tantra, Vedic rituals etc are done with a purpose in mind. These can be done for attaining Svarga Lokam. A person who is not settled tends to lose peace in the family. He keeps on changing Karma from one method to another. But after every failure, his mental condition goes from bad to worse.

Both Vidya (upasana) and Avidya (Karmas) are binding if they are practiced separately. If they are practiced together, one may transcend both to reach a state of better result.

Mantra 11

विद्यांचाविद्यांचयस्तद्वेदोभयंसह

अविद्यया मृत्युं तीर्त्वा विद्ययामृतमश्नुते 11

Vidyāṁ cāvidyāṁ ca

Yas tad vedobhayam saha,

Avidyayā mṛtyuṁ tīrtvā

Vidyayāmṛtam aśnute

Vidyam cha	= Vidya
Avidyam cha	= and Avidya
Ya	= he who
Tat vedobhayam	= Knows both
Saha	= together
Avidyaya	= by Avidya

Mrithyum	= death
Theerthva	= crossing
Vidyaya	= by Vidya
Amrutham Asnuthe	= enjoys freedom from sorrow

"He who knows and follows both Vidya and Avidya together overcomes death(sorrow) by Avidya and obtains happiness by Vidya."

We are now discussing Vidya and Avidya. Material activities[Karma] is Avidya and spiritual Upasana is Vidya. They are to be pursued together. Avidya alone can give the result of heaven[Svargam]. For that Karma has to be done perfectly. To attain heavenly bliss in this life and in the life after both Vidya and Avidya have a role. This would mean trying to attain long life, health and prosperity.

We all have a predestined life span. It is a journey. The idea is that the subtle body goes on after death and that the body is guided by its own Karma to come back to this world and attain a new body, a new life. Tendencies continue from life to life. We may continue as humans, Devas, animals, birds and so on.

Reincarnation is an inevitable belief of Indian philosophy and spirituality. Modern science need not support this. One who has faith in the scriptures is eligible to study the philosophy of reincarnation.

In Kathopanishad, Vajasravas performed a sacrifice called Visvajit. He had to offer all his wealth as Dana to whoever comes there. But unfortunately, the cows he kept for dakshina to priests were not up to the quality. Maybe all the good cows were already given away. This was noticed by his son Nachiketas who thought how he could overcome the unexpected crisis. He told his father that he considered himself as wealth which could be given to someone, and he wondered to whom he could be given. The result of his father's Yajna would be disastrous if it was flawed. The dakshina should make the priests happy. Otherwise, the Yajna itself is useless. But the father was furious and got irritated by his question and said "I am going to give you to Lord Yama, Lord of death". His father gave him to the lord of death, 'Yama'.

Nachiketas was welcomed at Yama's place and Yama, pleased with him, offered him three boons, which he could seek there itself. He used one of his boons to ask Yama about the journey of Atma and life after death. Only Shraddha, faith in the Scriptures and the words of Guru can help us to understand life and the life after.

Avidya or Karma is explained in Mundakopanishad 1.2.8 to 1.2.10th mantras.

Avidyayam bahudha varta mana:
Vayam krutartha ityabhimanyanti bala:'
Yat karmino na praveda yanti ragat
Thenathura ksheenalokaschya vanthe."(1-2-9)

Those following Avidya consider themselves as great because of the action they perform, but do not know that the result of their action comes to an end and they fall from heaven. He with desires present in his mind only falls miserably to the field of action. On exhaustion of the results of meritorious deeds (Punya) they fall down again to the field of action and sorrow. Actions good or bad give rise to limited results and hence there is a limitation to the satisfactions of the fruits of action. It may not be possible to fulfill all desires and reap the fruits of action in one birth. The individual may have to take several births for the sake of experiencing them.

Mundakopanishad 1-2-10 says

"Ishtapoortham manyamana varishtam
Nanyat shreyo vedayante pramooda:
Nakasya prushte te sukrutonubhootva
Imam lokam heenataram va vishanti."

Avidya leads one to heaven. After enjoying the pleasures there, when the merits of the Karma ceases, one is sent back. Following the path of Vidya and Avidya together when there is exhaustion of the sins, he attains Brahmalokam. Other than the heavenly worlds there are other worlds like Maharlokam, Thapolokam, Kailasom, etc where one can reach and have an extremely happy time. After the tenure of their stay at the higher realm, they may come back to this earth or go to a lower world where Asura rules. One can also return as an Asura (demon), a possibility that we have to be wary of. Examples are seen in texts like Ramayana, Bhagavatam etc.

One who traverses the different worlds is called a Samsari. These are the outcomes of following Vidya (upasana) and Avidya (Karma).

This is explained in Mundaka Upanishad 1-2-11.

'Tapasshradhe ye hyupavasanthyaranye,

Santa vidvamso bhaikshyacharyam charanta:

Soorya dvarena te viraja prayanti,

Yatramrita: sa Purusho Hyavyayatma'

Those who have sraddha, (accepting Veda as a Pramana) and practice a reclusive life with calmness of mind and Upasana and follow the lifestyle of a hermit, are freed from all unhappiness and traverse the passage through the sun to where that effulgent Lord Brahma resides.

Those under delusion that charities and sacrifices are the best, do not know anything better. Enjoying in heaven the fruits of the meritorious deeds, at the end of it they come back to the earth, or even to a lower world. Further, due to the absence of Punya and or accumulated Papa they may reach lower regions.

Mantra 12

अन्धंतमःप्रविशन्तियेऽसम्भूतिमुपासते

ततो भूय इव ते तमो य उ सम्भूत्यां रताः 12

andham tamah praviśanti

ye'sambhūtim uupāsat

tato bhuya iva te tamo

ya u sambhutyām ratāh

Antham	= blind
Tamah	= darkness
Pravisyanthi	= enter
Ye	= who
Asambhutim	= unmanifested, avyakruta

dhyana)

Upasate	= worship
Tato	= than
Bhuya	= greater
Iva	= as though
Te	= they
Sambhoothyam	= in the manifest,

(Saguna Brahmopasana)

Ratha   = devoted

They fall into pitch darkness who worship the unmanifest, Maya. They fall into greater darkness who devote themselves the manifest, Saguna Brahma."

These two words Sambhuti and Asambhuti are to be studied carefully. In the next mantra Sambhava and Asambhuti are mentioned. Sambhuti is manifested and Asambhuti is unmanifested. Sambhava means manifested and Asambhuti means unmanifested.

Above the Svargalokam is the Brahmalokam where Brahmaji resides. Above Brahmaji is the Moolaprakruti or Maya or Avyakrutam. As a consequence of Karma or upasana, one can reach Svargalokam or brahmalokam, or avyakrutam. Moolaprakruti and Brahmalokam are called Asambhuti and Sambhuti respectively. Sambhuti is manifested or brahmalokam. Asambhuti is unmanifested or Moolaprakruti. Moolaprakruti is anadi or eternal. Brahmalokam is not eternal. It was created or sambava or manifested. That which is created is destroyable also. Next mantra is about destruction. How can we attain Mulaprakriti or unmanifested?.

"Yoga chitha vritti nirodhaha" [second sutra(sentence) of Patanjali Yogasutra] means suspending the vrittis of chitta (antahkarana, including mind) in order to experience the ultimate reality and move towards self realization. Yoga means prevention of Chitta to form (Vrittis) and suspension of (Vrittis) formation. It is an effort until mind rests in a state of total and utter tranquility. Only such a person can reach moolaprakruti.

Yoga = definition of yoga is, Chitta= antahkarana (mind),

Vritti = fluctuations, Nirodaha= prevention, suspension or cessation

Chitta vritti is a term that refers to the appearance of antahkarana, mind in whatever the way. Chitta means antahkarana and vritti means appearance in this reference. We are aware of our surroundings –internal, external, physical or sensory world. It is the individual's unique awareness of one's thoughts, feelings, sensory experiences and environment. Chitha Vritti refers to the thought formation that takes place in the mind. We can reduce the thoughts and quieten the mind by increasing self- discipline and constant practice.

Five types of Vrittis are mentioned in the Yogasutra text. They are: Pramana, viparyaya, vikalpa, nidra and smrithi.

When a person is overcome with anger and becomes an angry person, physiological changes occur in the body internally and externally. Eyes become red. Facial expression changes. Speech is loud and unpleasant. Heart rate, blood pressure and respiratory rate increases, we do harmful acts also. But these thoughts are short lived. After some time, the angry thoughts are replaced by calm, loving thoughts. This is seen in all living beings. None can remain in the same thought for a long time. In the Puranas even Ravanan was found smiling, crying etc.

None can remain in the same chitta Vritti for a long time. Even Tapasvis (hermits) come out of their tapas. They show angry faces, happy faces. 'The thoughts' keep changing. As Patanjali Maharshi says in yoga sutra –the practice of yoga aims to control the vrittis of the chattering, fluctuating mind. So that we can reach the reality behind the thoughts.

Yoga chitta vritti Nirodhah is to stop all the thoughts and make the chitta free. All the thoughts have to be quietened, which is difficult. There should be a state where there are no thoughts, in such a state without sensory experiences and thoughts. But it is not the sleep state. Sleep is a state of mind without knowledge. A person practising chitta vritti nirodhah for a long time, at the time of death, leaving the physical body, he merges in the moolaprakruti, and that state is called moolaprakruti layam or being one with moolaprakruti, without any differentiation. Another name for Moolaprakruti is Avyakrutam.

All living beings, animate and inanimate objects can be traced to their primordial state. Existence of two eternal realities are mentioned in Shastra, they are Purusha and Prakruti. Both are indestructible. There are two aspects of prakruti. Sambhuti, the manifested and Asambhuti the unmanifested. Asambhuti or the initial state of Prakruti, a combined form of Trigunas (three gunas) and it is called primordial prakruti or moolaprakruti. In the moolaprakruti everything remains as unmanifest. When it expands at the time of creation, it becomes the subtle body of the universe. One who is in for reincarnation resides in the moolaprakruti. Vidya and Avidya indicate the paths and Sambhuti and Asambhuti as the final destinies. The person who chooses either, returns after his good deeds are over and he has to enter the cycle of birth and death. If he follows both together he reaches Brahmalokam, and thereafter attains Moksha. This is called kramamukti.

Mantra 13

अन्यदेवाहुःसम्भवादन्यदाहुरसम्भवात्

इति शुश्रुम धीराणां ये नस्तद्विचचक्षिरे 13

Anyadevahu: Sambhavat

AnyadahurAsambhutit

Iti susruma dhiranam

Ye na stad vichachakshire

Anyad	= different
Eva	= definitely
Sambhavat	= from the result of
	vyakruta
	or saguna Brahma
	upasana

Ahu:	= they say
Anyad	= different
Asambhutith	= from the result of avyakruta or Mula Prakriti

upasana

Iti	= thus
Sushruma	= we have heard
Dhiranam	= of the wise
Ye	= who
Na:	= to us
Vichachakshire	= explained

One thing, they say the result verily obtained from the worship of the Saguna Brahma is different. And the result of the worship of the Maya, Mula Prakriti is also different, thus have we heard from the wise who have explained to us.

This verse explains the knowledge of learned masters in the light of their experiences. Some yogis take the path of Asambhuti and some others take the path of Sambhuti. Asambhuti means the worship of one without attributes, nirguna, or formless. Sambhuti means the path leading to a personal God, Ishta Deva.

The Great Rishis are mentioned here by saying 'ye' (they) vichachakshire (taught us). Rishis are true investigators. They observe the entire life as a theme for their intense research and study. Every Rishi (seer, Saint, divine person, one who heard Veda directly from Isvara) had a strong relationship with their Gurus and later with their students. First guru is Isvara himself. Vedic life was followed and encouraged by kings of that era and now we are trying to understand and follow as much as we can and preserve the great masters' teachings.

Vidya and Avidya are complementary to each other. By the pursuit of desireless activity we can purify the mind in preparation for meditation. Later on the seeker gains the fulfillment through knowledge [Vidya].

MANTRA 14

सम्भूतिंचविनाशंचयस्तद्वेदोभयंसह

विनाशेन मृत्युं तीर्त्वा सम्भूत्यामृतमश्नुते

Sambhutim cha vinasham cha

Yastad vedobhayam saha

Vinashena mrtyum tirtva

sambhutya amrtamasnute

Sambutim ca	= avyakruta upasana and
Vinasham ca	= vyakruta upasana
Ya	= he who
Tad veda	= that knows
Ubhayam	= both
Saha	= together
Vinashena	= by following
	Sambhuti(Saguna Brahma)
Mrutyum teertva	= having crossed mrutyu
Asambutya	= by following

Asambhuti(Mula Prakriti)

Ashnute   = Enjoys

Amritham   = freedom from death

Vinasham or destruction is the same as Sambhava. The sambhuti is actually to be interpreted as Asambhuti. (Such usage is called "Aarsham" which means it is the freedom of Rishi to use the way it is). This is mentioned in Sankara bhashyam of Isavasya upanishad. Brahma Lokam is destined to be destroyed at the time of Pralaya, total destruction. Asambhuti means that which is not created otherwise called moolaprakruti.

One has to understand and follow the manifest and unmanifest, sambhuti and asambhuti, both at the same time, that includes Karma and upasana. Then the person who practices will attain a state which is totally unknown to ordinary people. It is a state of peace and non duality. This will remove fear of death as sloka says. Vinashena mrutyum theertva -he will be taught upanishad by Brahmaji himself when he is in brahmaloka and attain liberation.

Fear of death is manifested in many ways. I am destroyed, and what is mine is also going to be destroyed. That's how Mrutyu (death) is known to us. These two facts create fear in us. The thought of destruction brings misery. We do not like to think of these losses. But how to avoid death? This is only by acquiring knowledge about the practise of upasana. This Asambhuti upasana is for the attainment of Mula Prakriti. It enables us to attain absolute quietitude. To attain Mula Prakriti, one has to meditate upon Nirguna. This is possible for yogis. The yogis can reach this state by practicing Samadhi. This is possible only by the control of Prana and the Yogi's mind is absorbed in meditation, this is called Leena manasam. This is also to be accompanied with a high level of concentration and commitment.

mantra 15

हिरण्मयेनपात्रेणसत्यस्यापिहितंमुखम्

तत्त्वं पूषन्नपावृणु सत्यधर्माय दृष्टये 15

Hiranmayena patrena

satyasapihitam mukham

Thattvam pushannapavrnu

satyadharmaya drishtaye

The face of truth is covered by a golden lid. O Pushan, You may please (presiding deity in the form of sun) remove the lid for me, who is the follower of Dharma. May I realize the truth.

This is a prayer raised to the Lord Sun invoking his grace and blessing, so that the seeker may have the strength to remove the golden veil that hides the vision of truth. It implies the opening of the buddhi to the reality of Isvara and Atma.

This mantra highlights the search for truth. The previous mantra explained to us about Vidya, Avidya, Samboothi, Asamboothi, Sambavam, Vinasha and Asambhutim. The details of the spiritual

83

journey were highlighted. We shall review this once more.

Who am I ? What is the aim of life? We are all seeking peace and joy. Our need is to live peacefully in the time allotted. We all have several desires, irrespective of age or position. We expect our wishes to be fulfilled in our life. If we have no expectations that life will be dull and monotonous. Expectations give us the drive to go on. In other words, expectations help us to dream.

Even to dream we should have the ability and the eligibility to achieve it. For example, if I want to win a lottery of one million, I should buy a lottery ticket first. Not buying one will make me ineligible. We are all seeking permanent joy in the world and we work hard for the same. We must realize that the life of each one of us is running out day by day. Life is like lightning as far as the existence of the universe is concerned. We are all chalking out our future to get joy and peace in this life, and in life after death. We believe in life after death. Where to, is our journey after death? Is it to a higher, better world or is it to a lesser, worse world? Or do we reincarnate and come back to this world? Different religions have varied opinions about life after death. Even before religions came, people had varied opinions about life after death.

There are several questions, the answer to which we are all seeking. What will be our life span? What is the right path? How are we to cross samsara? Is there any pointer to lead us in the right path? The answers to all these questions are undoubtedly in the Vedas. We are blessed to be born in such a culture.

Vedas are the scriptures of Hinduism. All religions have their own scriptures detailing many aspects of life. But Vedas are the oldest scriptures. It is found to be about 10, 000 years old or more. Even the ancient Egyptian civilization is recognized to have originated in 3000 BC. Their pyramids have a lot of Egyptian writings, but these were not easily decipherable .

Vedas have always declared about the heavens and means for reaching the same. It's only thousands of years later that other religions came into being. The writings of the Vedas are in mantras. They have remained unchanged even after 10, 000 years in spite of there being nothing like intellectual property rights all these years. Once a mantra is revealed by a Rishi it cannot be changed in any manner by another person. The mantra continues several generations unchanged. Detailed inquiry tells us that it is because the mantras have a specific poetic composition called meters, it is called 'chandas' in Vedic literature. Even modern people cannot change it as there are special rules for reciting the mantras. 'Chandas' in Vedas means poetic meters. Example Gayatri mantra is a verse which has 8 letters in 3 rows. Total 24 letters. This verse is called Gayatri chandas. All the mantras similar to Gayatri chandas are called gayatri mantra. The way in which mantras are sung is called 'swara'. The different ways are called Udattam-high pitch, Anudattam-low pitch, Svaritam=in between high pitch and low pitch. Because the tunes, voice, sound, prose, poetry etc are all specific, the mantras can be sung only in one way. Any change would be detected at once. Thus the Vedas are always protected.

The Vedas have to be learned from teachers who are followers of the Vedic tradition. The pronunciation, tone, voice, etc. should be perfect and flawless. In the Vedas, there is a goal called the heaven or 'Svargam'. That's how humanity got the concept of heaven. Details of the journey to Svarga are elaborated. How long a person can exist there?. What are the paths? What happens afterwards? All is said in the Vedas. Other religions have their own way of explanations, that's why they are different. But the afterlife in heaven is not permanent . Once the merits are exhausted, we have to return to the earth to continue our journey. It is seen as a transitory phase for the righteous souls, who have done righteous deeds but are not ready for Moksha. "Ksheene punye martya lokam vishanti" [B.G. 9th chapter 21st sloka]

After explaining about Svarga, Upanishad explains about the people who are aiming to go there in mantras 11 to 14. It is said that the Karma yogis can reach Svargam. Karma yogi is one who does work in a prescribed manner by the Veda and fruits of Karma are dedicated to Isvara. It can be a 15 minute pooja or a one month long Yajna. This Karma will have a result. Both Karma and Karma phalam are not permanent. The punyam obtained by doing Karma does not last forever.

Both Vidya and Avidya (Karma) have a beginning and an end. It's a Karma being done by an individual. So the Karmaphalam also has an end.

Imagine there is a path in front of you. A lot of people are walking on this path. You also start. Soon the path forks into two. You are walking alone. One side is the path of Dharma or goodness. The other side is the path of adharma or evil which eventually leads to stealing, killing etc. The path of Dharma again forks into two. One goes to worldly Karma. This would include working for the betterment of society, family etc. The other path is the spiritual one.

If we walk along the spiritual path following the beliefs and practices or rather the path to the Supreme Power. We can have different intentions.

1. Attain Enlightenment.

2. Attain siddhis or supernatural power

3. Obtain high intellect

4. For a strong and healthy body

5. For a long life

An individual engaged in worldly life can get fed up with worldly affairs and turn to spirituality.

Some of us may think we are ignorant of Vedas. But actually, without knowing, we are reciting Vedas when we say Om. Reciting Om is the same as reciting Gayatri mantra. The Gayatri mantra is central to the Vedas. No need to have guilt of not worshiping Devatas or reciting mantras. It is approved in the Vedas to recite the name of Isvara like Sri Krishna or Sri Rama and at the end of every puja. You might have heard this - Narayanayeti samarpayami. It means all my actions, I surrender to Prabhu Sri Krishna, Narayana. This will release all sins accumulated through Karma.

In fact, many of our activities are related to spirituality. Literally it is like a Malayalee saying that he doesn't know Sanskrit. There are several words in Malayalam which are Sanskrit like Akasam, Vayu, Jalam, Agni etc. It is the same with all other Indian languages.

When we take the path of Dharma, which is decided by the individual, this includes the path of Vedic Karma and path of knowledge. The first path leads to Svargalokam, and path of knowledge to higher realms of reality. All those who reach Svargalokam do not reach the throne near to Indra. As per Purana, Pandu and some others had the privilege of getting that position. There are several realms in Svarga Loka upper and lower which an individual reaches as per his merits. This can be compared to a government office where there are several levels of positions like peon, clerk, director etc.

Those who follow the path of Vedic knowledge reach higher realms. There are many. First Svarga and above Svargaloka other Lokas (worlds) like Janalokam, Maharlokam, Tapolokam etc do exist. Those in higher realms rule over those in lower realms. Sidhas, Sadhyas and Gandharvas have special places there. These are the paths that can be followed.

There are several questions to be answered. Is it for this we are to learn Upanishads? Why are we not able to get happiness here? Why should we search for happiness in another place? I want happiness now itself. I want to be in a state of contentment where I don't need anything more. There are two paths presented in Vedanta. Path of knowledge and path of Karma. These two paths are different. What is gained by the path of knowledge cannot be gained by the path of Karma. There is only one path for Moksha, that is Jnanayoga. Karmayoga (the path of Karma) qualifies a person to get into the path of knowledge by removing obstacles for Brahma Jnana.

The Upanishads tell us the result of following the path of Karma. It tells us that by doing a particular Karma we will get result sooner or later. Isvara only knows the relationship between Karma and the result and he is the one who joins the Karma with the Karma phala (result). Every action done will have the desired result, that's what we want. When we talk about realization of God, how can we see a formless God with our eyes. We cannot experience God with our sense organs. As per Bhagavad Gita and Puranas we can understand God with our mind and intellect. It will become clear in our intellect, just like we understand the meaning of a word which is not seen with our eyes.

How is the Supreme Power to be realized in the intellect? Logically, Isvara is understood as the creator of the entire universe. We should understand how the universe came into being. Where is my origin? Why was I born? What is making us think in a particular way? Who controls the universe? Who decides what to happen when? Even this world will disappear one day. One who is reflecting over these questions would like to get the answer here in this life itself. The Upanishads declare that realizing the truth of the creation and creator in this life itself is desirable. If not understood now it will be disastrous. One who is of the opinion that he can go to the heavens and then see God there, he is called a 'moodda' (deluded, ignorant) or 'pramoodda' (the person with the highest level of confusion). These people have poor reasoning capacity. Anyone who takes an effort to realize that all that is here is Isvara, as Pujya Swami Dayananda Saraswati said, is praised in the Upanishads.

The Upanishads are meant for a person with intelligence who wants Moksha. To him, the Upanishad says "Hiranmayena Patrena Satyasa apihitam mukham." The Truth is covered by a golden plate. "Tat tvam pushan apavrunu." Invoking the Sun

God to remove the Golden Plate which covers the truth of Isvara. Praying to the Supreme to remove the veil of ignorance and show the Truth.

The Truth is covered by the Gold Radiance of the Sun. What we see is only the cover. We should see the radiance with our intelligence, not with our eyes which is a sense organ. I am praying to Isvara to remove the veil of ignorance and see the radiance inside me. Sun is the son of Prajapati. Sun is the source of light and energy for the entire solar system and in Vedic philosophy, the sun represents Surya Narayana Murthy.

When a person in deep concentration reaches a stage where there is loss of individual identity and at this dying moment of ignorance he prays to God to reveal truth to him. A prayer to transcend from darkness to light, a goal set as light being the symbol of realization of the supreme power. First two Mantras tell us about the Path of Jnanam and the path of Karmayoga to attain Moksha. In "Isavasyamidam sarvam" mentions about the path of Jnana and in "kurvanneveha Karmani" about the path of Karmayoga. From third mantra to fourteenth, the paths of dharma, Karma, and devotion leads to Brahmaloka and above that to Mula Prakriti as described. From 15th mantra onwards, the path of knowledge is given importance. "SatyadharMaya drishtaye" says follow the Truth in Principle. Path of righteous living and devotion belongs to the field of Karma. The doer-ship is there. This individual goes through happiness and sadness. He will be going via different paths to attain happiness and peace. From the view of Upanishads, all these come in the cycle of birth and death. All the spirituality we have followed is not as per Upanishad's direction. All these are Avidya and lead to darkness only. What we have to do to remove darkness and get realization is different from the path of Karma.

We all have a specific life expectancy. But we are ignorant of our life span. It can be cut off at any time. So in our short life span it is easier to follow the path of Karma and the path of devotion. Those who choose that reach Brahmalokam or Vaikuntam. They continue their life in the same way. When their merits are over they come back to enter into the cycle of birth and death. Other than these two paths (i.e.Karma and upasana), the Upanishads implore us to follow the path of knowledge. This is the path envisaged by Bhagavan Krishna in Bhagavad Gita. Bhagavan says

"SarvaDharman parityajya

Mamekam sharanam vraja

Aham twa sarva papebhyo

Mokshayikshyami ma shucha: (Gita 18.66)

Here Bhagavan tells Arjuna to renounce all Dharmas (Karma). There is an impression that following Dharma means a set of values like don't tell lies, don't be selfish etc. There is an impression that the Upanishads are filled with stories that uphold moral values like Panchatantra stories. A person who truly follows the path of knowledge like the Rishis has to be careful with what he does. Whatever is done by Rishis is Dharma only. But not that is for every other individual. So 'I am a Jnani, I can do anything' is not a good idea to follow. Therefore no need to worry about Dharma of Rishis. They are not tied to the world or society. They have detached themselves from all affairs of the world.

What is the difference between the path of knowledge and the path of devotion? All along, Sri Krishna was advising Arjuna to engage his mind in devotion and perform the duty as a warrior. He thus wanted Arjuna not to give up his Kshatriya Dharma and also follow the path of devotion along with this. This is the principle of Karma yoga.

Karma Sanyasa is renouncing all worldly duties. Yet here we may incur sin for abandoning our duties. So Karma Sanyasa is not advised. If you are a devotee and the goal is Moksha, then Prabhu Sri Krishna says not to fear. I will absolve you from all sins and liberate you from the samsara chakra. An example is the story of Parikshit, grandson of Arjuna.

Upanishads is a means of knowledge which frees us from all sins and miseries and leads us to peace, happiness and tranquility. Srividyopasana and Sakteyopasana are related to Tantrik method. The Upasana Murties have calm and angry expressions. Similarly even we have seen a Satvic person suddenly becoming angry, and his face expressions changing. The positive or negative outcome of an individual will depend on his basic mental frame and the experiences he has gone through. Based on this, the same person can be happy, sad, angry or peaceful. It is not possible to be always happy and radiating happiness to others. Just as our behavior changes off and on, we must realize that others are also like that. Their reaction to us can be pleasant or unpleasant based on whether we can influence them or not. But we have to be unchanged whatever be the circumstances and not to be like a ship without a rudder moving to and fro in the ocean. A spiritual person should be steady with a goal whatever the circumstances be. Such a person is called Karma yogi. He should have a firm knowledge about Jivatma and ParamAtma relationship.

The four goals of our life are Dharma [righteousness], Artha [wealth], Kama [pleasures], and Moksha [liberation]. The purpose of human life is to follow the law and lead a balanced life in which both material comforts and human passions have their own place and legitimacy. The four aims are necessary for the continuity of life on this earth and for the order of the world. Man cannot simply take birth on earth and start working for his salvation at once by means of Dharma alone. As he passes through the rigors of life and experiences human sufferings, he learns to appreciate the value of liberation. He then introspects about the purpose of life and Moksha.

Dharma has several meanings- duty, faith, righteousness, law, justice, ethics, morality. It is being responsible for order and harmony in the world. Material wealth plays an important role in overall happiness and well being of an individual. A householder needs wealth to perform his duties and to take care of the needs of his family and society. Desire for wealth is different from greed for wealth.

Kama means pleasure. To fulfill our desires wealth is needed. But this wealth has to be acquired on the pillars of Dharma. The science of Karma is called Dharma. This is explained in Meemamsa Sutras. It is also called Karma Meemamsa [Study of Vedic Karma]. Both Karma and Kama are closely connected to Dharma. Karma is action bringing about inevitable results good or bad in life or the life after. Whatever be the Karma [good or bad] it will have a goal.

Then what is the difference between man and animals?. Physically there is not much difference. They are also born, develop, grow, and later die. But their life is programmed. They don't have spiritual thoughts as far as we know. Their intellect doesn't change with the pattern of thoughts.

When a Jivatma comes into the world, it gets an appropriate body and is born to parents where its Karma phala can be exhausted. Jivatma can enter the word in any form. So in effect all living beings are similar in origin. We are not in any way superior to animals. Each one has its own life to complete.

We don't have the right to kill other animals for food, when we have many other alternatives. The energy of all food is from the sun. The plants utilize the energy and make food for all. From Brahmaji to a small blade of grass all have the same right to live with dignity. What rights do humans have to violate that? Each one takes birth to fulfill their Karmaphala and do their duty. The animal kingdom depends on each other. In the case of animals their habits are programmed. So they don't incur sin even when they kill and eat animals. E.g. tiger, Lion etc. But we incur sin when we kill or hurt other animals mentally or physically. If I kill an ant, I will incur sin. We have to repent later for this. It is envisaged in the Vedas that we have to be fair to all living beings. If not we will carry the demerit for several births. Contemplating over such thoughts will improve us as a human being, and this will be reflected in our relationship with all other living beings.

Next we shall see about Moksha, which should be the final goal of life. Moksha is freedom from ignorance and it is self realization. This is possible only by following the path of knowledge by the study of the Upanishads.

Next Mantra is a prayer for Moksha.

mantra 16

पूषन्नेकर्षेयमसूर्यप्राजापत्यव्यूह

रश्मीन्समूहतेजोयत्तेरूपंकल्याणतमं

तत्ते पश्यामि योऽसावसौ पुरुषः सोऽहमस्मि 16

Pushannekarshe Yama surya praajapatya

Vyuha rashmeen samooha tejo Yatte roopam kalyanatamam

tat te pashyami yo savasow purusha sohamasmi

Pushan = Oh the one who nourishes the world

Ekarshe = the one who moves alone and

Yama = the destroyer of all

Surya = the one who absorbs the essence of earth and living beings

Prajapatya = O son of Prajapati

Vyuha rashmeen = disperse rays

Sammooha teja = withdraw the power

Yat te Kalyanatamam = your most auspicious

Pashyami = I see

Ya: asou purusha: = this purusha

103

Sa aham asmi   = indeed I am.

The stanza is a direct prayer to Surya devata. All life on this earth is possible because of the inexhaustible radiance of the Sun. Yat te roopam kalyanatamam means we see your glorious nature. "Let me see the supreme power. So that all my sins are washed away". Knowledge requires removal of all our misconceptions, and we are able to understand the Supreme power, Isvara. Upanishads reveal to us the path to attain realization. Not just memorization of mantra, but by mental reflection and contemplation. Only contemplation and meditation of the mantra will lead us to the realization that each one of us is nothing but ParamAtma. This cannot be seen externally with our eyes. It is to be understood by repeated contemplation on the universal reality.

Mantra 17

वायुरनिलममृतमथेदंभस्मान्तंशरीरम्

ओं क्रतो स्मर कृतं स्मर क्रतो स्मर कृतं स्मर

Vayuranilam amrtam adhedam

bhasmantam sareeram

Om krato smara krutam smara

krato smara krutam smara

(Gachatu)Vayu   = let go
Prana

Amrutam Anilam   = to devata
of

                                                                universal
air

Atha   =there after

Idam bhasmantam sareeram   = this body
may

                                                                reduced   to
ashes

Krato smara   = O mind

                                                                remember

Krutam smara   = remember
deed

Let my prana merge into Vayu devata and let
this body be burnt by fire to ashes 'Om' O! mind
remember. Remember what you have done."

At the time of death, let my prana merge with Vayu Devata and let my body go back to the ashes. May I remember all that was done in the past. This mantra is a prayer at the time of dying. Let the last breath of air join and become one with the all pervading air. Krato means oh! mind. Let us remember our most intense experiences which should be the unforgettable experience of the absolute.

Mantra 18

अग्नेनयसुपथारायेअस्मान्विश्वानिदेववयुनानिवि

द्वान्

युयोध्यस्मज्जुहुराणमेनो भूयिष्ठां ते नमउक्तिं

विधेम

Agne naya supatha Raye asman

Visvani Deva vayunani vidvan

Yuyodhyasmajjuhurana mena:

bhuyishtam te nama uktim vidhema

agni! Naya   = O agni lead

Asman   = us

Supatha Raye = good path To wealth

Deva = O Deva

Vishvani vayunani vidvan = knower who knows all the ways

Yuyodhi = remove, separate

Juhuranam ena: = this deceptive sin

Te = to you

Bhooyishtam = again and again, very much

Nama uktim vidhema = we do say namaste

"O Agni! Lead us on to the right path to the field of wealth, as you are the one who knows all means to obtain that. Here wealth is Karmaphala, results of action. Remove the deceptive or cheating sin (which prevents the departing soul to the heaven) from us. We offer our best salutations in words."

Here in this stanza Lord Agni (fire) has been invoked to lead to the higher level of heaven which is not available by ordinary Karma. In our ancient Vedic literature, we find mention of two paths taken by the Jivatma after death. One is Dhuma marga, the path beginning with smoke and associated with the moon and Dakshinayana. Dakshinayana refers to the six month period between summer solstice and winter solstice beginning with July 16, when the sun moves towards the southern Hemisphere. The other is Archiradi marga, the path beginning with flame and associated with sun and Uttarayana. The Sun starts moving towards the northern Hemisphere. These paths are called Pitrayana and Devaayana respectively. The first path is to Pretalokam, or the world of death, where Lord Yama rules, and second path is to Svargaloka, which is ruled by Indra, the lord of Devas.

Here in this mantra we invoke Agni Deva to lead us to Deva Loka. "Yuyodhyasmajjuhuranamenam" (yuyodhi asmad juhuranam enam) Please destroy the sins in me. The individual finally yields up himself to God in an inward salutation. "bhuyishtam te nama uktim vidhem" I salute you again and again.

पूर्णमदः पूर्णमिदं पूर्णात्पूर्णमुदच्यते

पूर्णस्य पूर्णमादाय पूर्णमेवावशिष्यते

om शान्तिः शान्तिः शान्तिः

Om   purnamadahpurnamidam
purnatpurnamudacyate

Purnasyapurnamadaya
Poornamevaavashishyate

Om shanti sshanti sshanti

Jennifer H. Catto

Swami Turya Chaitanya has asked for some notes about myself, so I will share a bit of information here. I live in the western United States and was raised in a fairly secular household with a casual connection to spirituality and religion. Going to church was more of a social activity in our family than a devotional undertaking. Later, I studied literature and journalism in college and worked for a number of years in television production and radio newscasting. As my children grew, I became more and more interested in spirituality in general and non duality specifically, having been blessed with shraddha in the truth of non duality, the spiritual oneness of everything, from a fairly young age. After exploring various teachers from the west on the topic for several years, I was introduced to the teachings of the Upanishads and the Bhagavad Gita by some like minded Western friends, who also introduced me to the writings of Swami Dayananda Saraswati, which have been such a great blessing in my life.

I am grateful to several informed and qualified teachers who have helped with my studies, and I am very grateful to have met Swamiji Turya and to have shared some of Swami Dayananda's teachings – with Swami Turya's blessings – to an international on-line group of Vedanta students.

For Vedanta, in addition to the study of the Upanishads and some ancillary texts such as Drig Drishya and Vivekachudamani, the study of the Bhagavad Gita is invaluable and essential. And, as expressed in the Bhagavad Gita, the practice of Karma Yoga is an important devotional and purifying practice. In Karma Yoga, we learn to dedicate all our actions to God, and to take the result of the actions as a gift. As Swami Dayanandaji says, the results may be greater than what we expect, the same as what we expect, less than what we expect, or the opposite of what we expect. But no matter the type of result, when the result is understood to be a gift from Isvara — a gift that is in keeping with universal laws – one comes to grow in maturity. Also, the inner instrument of the mind/emotions becomes purified, and more ready for further spiritual study and assimilation.

Some Vedanta teachers have told me that perhaps I was an Indian in a prior lifetime, and I don't argue the point! Perhaps that is why I recognized the validity of these teachings so readily when first exposed to them.

In any case, I am very grateful to the spiritual heritage of India, the teachings of the Vedas, and the teachings and teachers of Vedanta. Vedanta is a means of knowledge used to discover the truth of oneself as limitless, whole and complete. As it turns out, everything we do in life, all our struggles and endeavors on every front, are an attempt to search for this wholeness, a wholeness that we already are. With the blessing of the teachings, one comes to recognize this fact, and to make one's contributions from a sense of fullness and completion, rather than for a sense of fullness and completion.

Namaste to all,

Jennifer H. Catto

Dr Latha Pillai

As an inquisitive young girl who was exposed to the teachings of Swami Chinmayanandaji ,I have been inspired by the Bhagavat Gita and Upanishads .I am a voracious reader and a pediatrician by profession. I always had the spark in me to attend any discourses on the Bhagavat Gita and Upanishads. I had the privilege to be a part of Vedanta course. I thank Dr Mini Pillai my good friend for introducing me to Swami Turya Chaitanyaji. I am thankful to my Parents,Husband Dr, Ajay and my children for their unstinting support. I am deeply contented that I could be a part of His Holiness Swami Turya Chaitanyaji in his effort to spread the teachings of Hinduism.

Dr Latha Pillai

Ramakrishnan Karivellur

I was born in North Malabar region of Kerala where learning of spiritual texts are very difficult. My place is a fort of Communism and atheism. Majority of the Hindus of my area are communists and atheists. I too was brought up in this way and started talking against Ishwara and Spirituality like others. I worked in Kerala Health Service Department and did my service to the country and now leading a retired life. It was my fortune that I met revered Swami Vimuktha Chaitanyaji, and Swami Vineeth Chaitanyaji. Swami Vimukthaji initiated me in to spirituality and taught me Tattva Bodha text in a detailed way. During the period I met Swami Nirmalanda Giri Maharaj and started attending his classes. This made a fundamental change in me and I was attracted in the wisdom of spirituality. I met Swami Turyachaitanyaji at that time and started attending his classes also. I attended almost all classes of Swami Turyaji while he was at Malabar during 1990's. I met H.H. Swami

Dayananda Saraswathi and received blessings when he visited Payyannur by the initiative of Swami Turyaji. Later when Swami Turyaji left Kannur and I too lost connection with spiritual classes and literally came to an end of my spiritual persuit. It is a miracle and blessings of Ishwara that after 25 years I met Swami Turyaji at Eranakulam and every weekend I started coming from Kannur to Kochi Ashram of Swamiji. Again I started my spiritual persuit in a more comfortable way. As part of my spiritual sadhana I started writing class notes and Swamiji told me to write and share with others. That made me to complete this work and many other works. I have already written "Purusha Sukta", "Gayathri Mantra" and "Drik Drisya Viveka". When Swamiji started Bhagavad Geeta, that is my current project and first chapter is already completed. I pray to Lord Dakshina Murthy to bless all mumukshus and bless all of us with Brahma Jnana.

Hari Om. Tat Sat.

Ramakrishnan Karivallur

Ganga Ramamurthy

Born into a family where rituals, prayers and devotional songs played an essential part, I grew up with great devotion and love for God . When I joined Chinmaya Vidyalaya as a teacher, it was then that I was first introduced to The Bhagavad Gita.I was blessed to attend Swami Chinmayananda's Bhagavad Gita Jnana Yajnam and Morning classes on Mandukya Upanishad. This opened the wider vista for me and my search for Truth started. In the course of our journey as seekers(I say 'our' because I am fortunate to have none other than my husband as my companion guiding and encouraging me) we met a couple Shri. M. Ramachandran and Smt.Devaki who were already in this quest. It was in their house that we first met Turya Swamiji. My actual interaction with Swamiji started coincidentally on August 15th! We were lucky to meet him in person and I remember asking Swamiji, " When in meditation, and for some time after that, we can feel the peace, but at the slightest disturbance we are back to square one!

How can we always remain in that peaceful state?".
Well, Swamiji said "when you realize you are what
you are seeking!". I was intrigued and then started to
attend Swamiji's classes in The Bhagavad Gita,
Upanishads and also Sanskrit Grammar. We were
also fortunate to be in Swamiji's presence in informal
gatherings, when Swamiji would impart some very
deep insights to us. My search ended under Swamiji's
tutelage. The journey continues…

Hari Om.

With Pranams

Ganga

Dr Mini G Pillai

दुर्लभं त्रयमेवैतद्दैवानुग्रहहेतुकम् ।

मनुष्यत्वं मुमुक्षुत्वं महापुरुषसंश्रयः ॥ ३ ॥

These are three things which are rare
indeed and happen due to the grace of God - a human

birth, the longing for Liberation, and the protecting care of a great teacher.

In the worldly sense, it is by chance that myself and my husband, Sri K Ramesh came into touch with Swamiji and through him, with Pujya Swamiji Dayananda Saraswati; but seekers would definitely recognise the divine design in getting a teacher who is keen to impart knowledge.I am an endocrinologist by profession and is working at Ernakulam. Blessed to be Swami Turya Chaitanyaji's student for the last 12 years.

Dr   Mini.G.Pillai   MD   (General Medicine),DNB(Endocrinology)   Consultant Endocrinologist,

This book is released on 15th August 2021 on the occation of Pujya swami Swami Dayananda Saraswathi ji 's birthday.

Sri Ramesh